Contents

Total war

Yes, we were married on 3 September 1939. The day war broke out. It was a rushed job and, I suppose, a rather romantic gesture. But we thought that we weren't going to live much longer, so we might as well get married while we could. You see, the boffins had predicted that 10,000 people a day would be killed in the air raids alone. There weren't going to be many people left in Britain after a while. It was going to be total war.[1]

IN THE EVENT, the scientists were wrong in their estimates of the number of British casualties the war would bring. Mr Widdowson and his wife Jane survived the war and still live happily in the house they moved into on their wedding day. But the memories of their first six years of married life are forever etched on their minds. The couple were part of Britain's home front.

Until the twentieth century most wars were relatively small-scale, particularly for the British. The civilian population was not unduly affected. With the First World War (1914–18) this changed. All able-bodied men had to join the armed forces. At home people had their food and other goods rationed, and

Even before war was declared, precautions were being taken to protect important buildings in the major cities. The heavy sand-filled bags stacked against the building were designed to shield windows and doors from bomb blast.

Witness History Series

11119

THE HOME FRONT

Stewart Ross

Wayland

Titles in this series

Cover illustration: A recruitment poster for the Auxiliary Fire
Service.

First published in 1990 by
Wayland (Publishers) Ltd
61 Western Road, Hove
East Sussex BN3 1JD, England

Editor: Heather Ancient
Series editor: Catherine Ellis
Designer: Ross George
Consultant: Terry Charman, researcher and historian at
the Imperial War Museum.

British Library Cataloguing in Publication Data
Ross, Stewart
The home front.
1. Great Britain. Social conditions. Effects of world war
2
I. Title
941.084

ISBN 1–85210–868–1

Typeset by Rachel Gibbs, Wayland
Printed in France by G. Canale & C.S.p.A., Turin
Bound in France by A.G.M.

▲ A Home Guard soldier relaxing at home between spells of duty. What item in the picture suggests that he thought it necessary to be ready for action at any time?

◄ The war affected every aspect of civilian life on the home front. Even children's games and toys reflected the conflict.

they found restrictions and deprivations altering several other aspects of their lives. War had become 'total', involving everyone, all the time. As well as the soldiers at the battle front, there was now a home front in which all citizens were expected to play their part in helping to win the war.

In the Second World War (1939–45) the home front was even more important than it had been in the First World War. This time there was a serious threat of invasion, so a

Home Guard was formed. The threat of air raids led to the evacuation of mothers and children from the cities, a black-out was established and thousands of bomb shelters were constructed. The government directed the lives of all people in an unprecedented manner, controlling work, food, travel and leisure. Many women found new freedoms as they were recruited into the factories and earned their own wages for the first time. Everything, from radio programmes to railway travel, was geared to the war effort. If the home front crumbled, the war would be lost.

Of course Britain was not the only country with a home front. Every nation involved in the war found that the hostilities affected life far away from the battlefields. The situation in each country was different; many people found their country occupied by hostile foreign troops.

1

DEMOCRACY SUSPENDED
Churchill's government

SINCE 1928, WHEN all women were finally given the right to vote on the same terms as men, Britain had been a representative democracy. Local and central governments were elected. Traditions and laws guaranteed British citizens certain basic freedoms, such as the right to free speech, a fair trial and enjoyment of their own property. In 1939 and 1940 many of these measures and safeguards were suspended for the duration of the war, giving the government almost complete control over people and property.

When war broke out Prime Minister Neville Chamberlain set up a small war cabinet to direct the nation's affairs. New ministries were established for Food, Shipping, Economic Warfare and Information. This last department was really responsible for propaganda, but the government did not like the sound of a word which had overtones of brainwashing; besides, the German Reich had a Ministry of Propaganda. The government used its powers to enforce a variety of measures they considered essential. Suspected foreigners

An official poster which caused some controversy and ill-feeling when it appeared in 1939. Do you think it appears to be asking the people to win a victory for the government?

Winston Churchill inspecting
the Channel defences shortly
after he was appointed prime
minister in 1940.

were locked away without trial, all men up to the age of forty-one were liable to conscription, and at night there were to be no lights visible anywhere in case they attracted German bombers. (As the ban on car lights led to a doubling of road deaths in September 1939, the regulations were relaxed to allow drivers one restricted headlamp.)

There was little fighting on land during the first seven months of the war. The period became known as the 'bore' or 'phoney' war when the major nations, in Churchill's words, stood facing each other in a 'sinister trance'. People began to question the need for the strict government measures. They were annoyed by posters like the one shown on page 6 which seemed to divide the nation between 'you' and 'us', the people and their government.

The war suddenly became real when the Germans invaded western Europe in April and May 1940. Chamberlain's spiritless leadership was rejected and Winston Churchill was chosen to replace him. Although Churchill said that he had nothing to offer but 'blood, toil, tears and sweat', he was an inspiring and respected figure.

Chamberlain remained in Churchill's war cabinet. He was joined by Lord Halifax (Conservative) and the Labour MPs Clement Attlee and Arthur Greenwood. Churchill soon appointed his friend Lord Beaverbrook as Minister of Aircraft Production and Ernest Bevin (Labour) as Minister of Labour. The Emergency Powers Act, rushed through Parliament in three hours on 22 May, gave the new cabinet unlimited powers to conduct the war.

Loyal opposition

The famous Zec cartoon from the *Daily Mirror*, March 1942. The home secretary thought it was criticizing the price rise which had just been announced. Is the cartoonist's message clear?

"The price of petrol has been increased by one penny."—Official.

During the course of the Second World War no general election was held in Britain. In theory there should have been an election in 1940, five years after the last one, but it was felt that it would be unwise to encourage disagreement within the nation during wartime. By-elections were allowed to take place, although few of them were hotly contested because the major political parties had agreed to an electoral truce.

Churchill's government was a coalition, made up of members of both the Conservative and Labour parties, with one Liberal and two National Liberals. Nevertheless, in the House of Commons there was always some opposition to the government, mainly from left wing Labour MPs. Democracy, though suspended, was not completely abandoned. It would have been strange if it had, for the war was fought to preserve a free society.

One of the best-known examples of how Churchill continued to allow his government to be challenged in Parliament, despite even more pressing threats from the Germans and

Japanese, came in July 1942. The war had gone badly, with heavy defeats for Britain in the Far East. Concerned MPs asked that this motion be debated in the House of Commons:

> . . . that the House, while paying tribute to the heroism and endurance of the armed forces of the Crown in circumstances of exceptional difficulty, has no confidence in the central direction of the war.[2]

Some MPs did not want the debate to take place at such a crucial time in the nation's history. Churchill replied:

> This Vote of Censure has been on the Order Paper for some time and it has been flashed all over the world . . . Now that this has gone so far it would be in my opinion even more injurious to delay a decision than go forward with its issue.[2]

Why do you think that Churchill felt that to cancel the debate would do more harm than letting it take place? At the end of two days' debate his government won the vote by a majority of 451.

However, although opposition to the government was permitted in Parliament, very little was tolerated outside. In 1941 Home Secretary Herbert Morrison closed down the communist newspaper, the *Daily Worker*, for being too defeatist. It believed the war to be a capitalist plot. A year later Morrison almost did the same to the *Daily Mirror* when it published the cartoon by Zec shown on page 8. Morrison thought that the artist was attacking the profits of the oil companies. Zec claimed to be urging people to use petrol carefully as sailors were risking their lives to bring it to them. What do you think is the cartoonist's message?

▲ The Houses of Parliament after they had been hit by a German bomb. Do the people examining the damage seem unduly concerned?

◀ Churchill included politicians from all the major parties in his coalition government. Here the Labour MP Ernest Bevin is talking to dock workers.

9

Under the Nazi heel

In several ways the home front in Germany was similar to that in Britain. The Germans experienced censorship, conscription, rationing and black-out. There were no elections and much of the national effort was geared to winning the war. However, the Nazi system was much more extreme than that in Britain. The state was in total control of all the media. It was inconceivable for politicians or the military leaders to be criticized in the way they were in Britain. There was no free parliament in Germany, and opposition parties were not even allowed to exist.

Life on the German home front became even harsher after the Nazi Propaganda Minister, Dr Goebbels, introduced measures for 'total war'. He recorded in his diary:

> September 29, 1943. We are now carrying out my idea of 'total war'. We are stopping the production of anything that does not help us in the war. This means that another 8,000,000 workers can go into making things for the war, and 300,000 other workers will now be able to join the army. All factories will soon be making war materials.[3]

Many simple objects like pots and pans, bathplugs and pencils were no longer manufactured for civilian use. Similarly in

UNDER THE NAZI HEEL
Extent of Nazi and Axis Occupation 1939-41

ICELAND
NORWAY
SWEDEN
FINLAND
ESTONIA
LATVIA
LITHUANIA
DENMARK
EAST PRUSSIA
RUSSIA
UNITED KINGDOM
IRISH FREE STATE
HOLLAND
BELGIUM
GERMANY
POLAND
SLOVAKIA
FRANCE
AUSTRIA HUNGARY
SWITZ
ROMANIA
VICHY FRANCE
ITALY
YUGOSLAVIA
BULGARIA
ALBANIA
PORTUGAL
SPAIN
GREECE
TURKEY
MOROCCO
ALGERIA
TUNISIA
LIBYA
EGYPT

In 1941 the huge Nazi empire, which dominated Europe, stretched from the Atlantic to the Russian border.

Britain the government banned the issue of pencil sharpeners to the Civil Service as a way of saving pencils.

In 1943 the Nazi intelligence service was reporting that:

> . . . the telling of vulgar jokes against the state, even about the Führer himself, has increased considerably.[4]

Do you think that Goebbels' 'total war' raised or lowered the morale of the German people? Do you think the deprivations the work-force suffered affected their performance at work?

It is probable that Churchill's government was wise to allow some criticism to be made of its policies. This enabled it to find out what people were thinking and do its best to meet their needs. Because open criticism was forbidden in Germany in the end some people grew desperate, and attempts were made to kill Hitler:

> The assassination must be attempted at any cost. We must prove to the world and to future generations that the men of the German Resistance dared to take the decisive step and risk their lives on it.[5]

Do you think it is significant that, even when the war was going badly for them, the British never spoke about Churchill in these terms?

▲ Adolf Hitler at a Nazi rally in 1938. He was assured of an enthusiastic reception from the crowd at such events.

▼ Harvesting potatoes in the centre of Berlin in 1948. Such hardship was not part of Hitler's plan for the glorious future of the German people.

2
LIFE GOES ON
Wartime Britain

I had no idea what the word 'war' meant, nor why I said 'I hope there won't be a war, Mummy.'
She made no reply; I was not reassured. A few minutes later, the prime minister's voice was heard on the radio. The dreadful unknown war had just begun. I was desperate. I went out into the street, in search of comfort. I found nothing but the fear on people's faces.[6]

THESE WERE THE thoughts of a girl aged nine when war broke out. Like many other people, she did not know what the war would bring.

For everyone on the home front the experience of war was different. For some it meant total boredom, stuck in a dull, routine job. For others, who lost relatives and possessions, it brought deep misery. For many, however, the war was an exciting, challenging experience. One man recalls:

Oh yes! They were the best days of my life. Everyone was carefree and uninhibited. There was a great sense of comradeship. Everyone helped each other.[7]

Many people remember how everybody seemed to pull together to achieve a single goal – defeat of the enemy.

Whatever a person's experience of the

Why do you think these signposts were removed when it was thought the Germans might invade Britain?

Hitler will send
no warning –
so always carry
your gas mask

▲ Government posters encouraged people to always be prepared for a gas attack. As it turned out, neither side was prepared to use this terrible weapon on civilians.

▶ Constructing a black-out in London's Westminster Hospital. Blacking-out made it difficult for enemy bombers to find their target.

conflict, it could not be avoided. Here is an extract from a book published just after the war. Consider the meaning of the last phrase, which the author has emphasized:

> Life on the home front in modern war was life lived under conditions new in the history of our land. Every phase of it felt the direct influence of the total conflict . . . goods were manufactured, books were written . . . crops were grown, plans for trading . . . were . . . executed, industrial, religious and social affairs were carried on, mass transfers of population were made, and the business of government administered, not at some remote base from which the fighters had been sent, **but on the battlefield itself**.[8]

The war was brought home to people at once by the black-out, the need to carry a gas mask wherever one went, and conscription. Identity cards, rationing of food and fuel, shortages, and restrictions on almost everything, and the requirement for everyone to help in the national effort soon ensured that the home front was well and truly at war.

The sinews of war

The most vital work on the home front was the manufacture of food and weapons of war. The production of armaments was particularly important because when the British Army retreated from Dunkirk in 1940 they abandoned all their equipment. The loss of merchant vessels through attacks from German submarines and surface raiders was also considerable: 13½ million tonnes of shipping were sunk in the war, equivalent to 'almost two-thirds of the total British merchant fleet in September 1939.'[9] These ships had to be replaced and their numbers added to.

Government money poured into defence spending; a budget of £254.4 million in 1938-9 rose to £5,125.0 million in 1944-5. As a proportion of all government expenditure this was a rise from 21.45 per cent to 82.94 per cent.[10] Industrial output rose dramatically. Between the end of 1939 and the first months of 1943 small-arms and shell manufacture rose tenfold, gun output seven-and-a-half times, and the production of wheeled vehicles three-and-a-half times. Britain had three times as many aircraft in 1944 as in 1939, and ten times as many bombers.[11]

How was the increased production achieved? The Minister of Labour had the power to order anyone to work in any job where he or she was required. People without family ties were moved all over the country, and employment was found for those without work. By the end of 1942, 22 million people between the ages of 14 and 65, out of a total of 33 million, were in some form

British merchant vessels in a convoy, escorted by the Navy. It was vital that supply ships should reach Britain safely. What were the advantages for such ships travelling together rather than alone?

HOUSEWIFE: 1944

The Hand that held the Hoover works the Lathe!

With no glamour of uniform, with all the burdens and responsibilities of running a home, thousands of housewives in 1944 are war-workers too. They are doing a double job. They get no medals for it. But if ever women deserved especial honour, these do. So to all war-workers who also tackle shopping queues, cooking, cleaning, mending and the hundred and one other household jobs

Salute! FROM HOOVER

Hoover users know best what improvements they would like in the post-war Hoover. Suggestions are welcome.

BY APPOINTMENT TO H.M. KING GEORGE VI AND H.M. QUEEN MARY
HOOVER LIMITED. PERIVALE, GREENFORD, MIDDLESEX

This Hoover advertisement of March 1944 reflected the change in the way many women viewed themselves during the war.

of work to further the war effort.[12] Premises were requisitioned by the government and turned over to war work. For example, the Littlewoods pool and mail order business was used for the construction of barrage balloons. Hours of work increased: men in aircraft factories had to work ten hours a day for seven days a week. Safety regulations were allowed to lapse a little; as a result of this several women unused to factory work were scalped when their long hair caught in the machinery.

By 1944 Germany was using the forced labour of over seven million prisoners and imported foreign workers. Yet, with fewer resources, British industrial production outstripped that of the enemy. How was this achieved? Perhaps one explanation was people's eagerness to help in the war effort. Consider the following comments by a woman who could not work because she had three small children. She felt it was:

> *. . . humiliating . . . to realize that one was considered the lowest form of human life, of no use to the government, to the war effort, or to the ARP [Air Raid Precautions].*[13]

Everyone, who could, wanted to help in the war effort.

The workers

During the Second World War the work-force was more carefully organized in Britain than in any other country. All men and women had to register, and those who were not in 'reserved occupations' could be placed in the armed forces or in industry. By the end of the war there were 780,000 in the navy, one million in the RAF and 3 million in the army. Millions of others held part-time positions in the ARP, the Home Guard or one of the other organizations created by the war. The number of people in employment rose by 2.9 million between 1939 and 1943, but there was still a shortage of labour in key industries.

Two reservists studying the call-up poster issued on 4 September 1939. By mid-1943 every able-bodied person was required to register for war work. Why do you think that there was little resistance among Britons to this order?

Compare the pay of those in the forces (up to 1944) with factory workers:

Soldier – 14s (£0.70) per week with food and accommodation.
Soldier's wife – £1 5s 0d (£1.25) per week, but the husband's pay was reduced to 7s (35p) per week.
Female factory trainee – £1 18s 0d (£1.90) per week.
Male factory trainee – £3 0s 6d (£3.02½) per week.
Male factory worker – up to £7 0s 0d (£7.00) per week.

Now consider the weekly household expenses of a working class family of five, suggested in the *Daily Express* of 31 May 1940:

Rent	10s 6d	(£0.52½)
Coal	4s 4d	(£0.21½)
Gas and electricity	3s 6d	(£0.17½)
Insurance	4s 8d	(£0.23½)
Clothes	3s 0d	(£0.15)
Food	£1 10s 0d	(£1.50)
Sundries	4s 0d	(£0.20)
Total	£3 0s 0d	(£3.00) [14]

A poster urging women to join the Auxiliary Territorial Service because drivers were in short supply.

The low wages of ordinary men and women in the armed services were raised only in 1944. What effect do you think the poor pay might have had on morale? Why do you think a man described his friend who had failed the army medical fitness test as a 'lucky devil'?[15] Was it just that his friend would be safer at home?

Perhaps the luckiest of all were those in the reserved occupations. These included certain business men, farmers, doctors, dentists, nurses and skilled workers in key industries. They were able to continue with their work as before the war.

A total of 60,000 people (2,000 women and 58,000 men) objected to joining the forces on grounds of conscience. Some were pacifists, others were forbidden to fight by their religion. All had to go before tribunals to explain their objections. Of these 40,000 were told to take up useful employment, such as agriculture; about 5,000 went to prison; the rest were permitted to go free. Would you have been prepared to fight?

Feeding the people

'We never starved', remembered one Tyneside boy of his war years,

> . . . but we ate some bloody funny things. Best was American dried egg. You poured a thin trickle into the frying pan, then . . . it blew up . . . like a big yellow hump-backed whale.[16]

A girl recalled:

> I can remember the state our whole estate was in when the Co-op got a box of bananas. Everyone queued up for hours. My mam dragged me into the shop with her. Just one banana and we had to wait all day. I was really bored.[17]

Some children never saw bananas at all. When they were first given to boys at a boarding school, for a joke the pupils were asked to save the skins so that they could be refilled: at the end of the meal the boys obediently handed in all the skins to a bewildered master!

Britain was not able to produce enough food to feed the whole nation. Although during the war 2.75 million hectares of additional land were under the plough, food still had to be imported from abroad, much of it from North America. Since as many ships as possible were needed to transport military materials, shortages were inevitable and food was rationed.

Each person was given a ration book which contained coupons that were removed

► **(Top) A London park being converted to agriculture. People were urged to 'Dig for Victory'.**

► **(Bottom) This poster reminded people that they had to register in order to receive meat coupons.**

◄ *'Nothing but money, money, money! Where the blazes do they keep their coupons?'* **Why do you think the thief in this cartoon wants coupons rather than money?**

MINISTRY **⟨crest⟩** OF FOOD

REGISTER NOW
FOR
MEAT

YOU must register now to enable the Ministry of Food to

distribute meat fairly to the shops throughout the country,

and to assure YOU of your fair share when rationing begins.

WHAT YOU HAVE TO DO NOW :—

1 Put your name and address on the counterfoil at the bottom of the Meat Page of your Ration Book NOW.　**2** Write on the inside front cover of your Ration Book the name and address of your butcher.

3 Take your Ration Book to your butcher and let him write his name and address on the meat counterfoil and cut it out.

4 If you move to another district, take your Ration Book to the local Food Office in your new district.　**5** The numbered coupons *must not* be cut out yet. This will be done by your butcher when you do your shopping after meat rationing begins.

6 If you have registered for meat before Christmas, this registration was unauthorised. You may let it stand, and it will then be effective. Or, if you wish, you may register now with another butcher by recovering the counterfoil from the butcher who holds it and taking it to the butcher you now choose.

YOU ARE FREE TO CHOOSE ANY BUTCHER YOU LIKE

YOU MUST REGISTER NOT LATER THAN

MONDAY 8TH JANUARY

when goods were purchased. In 1943 the weekly allowances per person were: butter 57g, margarine 104g, cooking fat 57g, sugar 226g, tea 57g, cheese 28g and jam 450g a month. Meat was rationed by value, at 1s 2d (6p) a week. Other foods, such as tinned fish, fruit and biscuits, were allocated on a points basis. Each person was permitted goods worth 20 points a month. A tin of processed meat was worth 16 points. What were the advantages of rationing food?

Home-grown food was usually in plentiful supply and the papers were full of new, but not always very appetizing, ways to cook the left-overs. On 30 August 1940, the *Daily Mirror* had recipes for cabbage stalks, the outer leaves of cabbage and stale bread.[18] White bread was unavailable as it was more expensive to produce than wholemeal bread.

As you may imagine, there was a flourishing trade in stolen food. The government called this the Black Market and tried unsuccessfully to stop it. Despite the shortages, the population was healthier during the war than it had been before. If you consider the types of food that were available and those that were in restricted supply can you work out why?

Making do

Due to rationing and shortages of supplies, queuing for food became a normal way of life for British people.

It is difficult for us to imagine how people survived on the home front during the long years of the war. So many of the things that we take for granted were simply not available, or were in very short supply. How would you and your family cope if the following were almost unobtainable: cutlery, underwear, shoe polish, combs, bedding, razor blades, furniture, petrol, shoes? This is only a selection of items. There were many others, including most types of food and clothes, that were tightly rationed.

One explanation of why the nation managed is that even before the war many people's standard of living was very low. Surveys produced the following results: in some parts of London one-quarter of the population lived in poverty; in Bristol the figure was one-fifth; one-third of the working class in York had insufficient income to live on.[19] The war actually benefited many of these people. The need to work together in the face of hardship helped break down some class barriers and revealed to the better off the extent of the deprivation suffered by others. Rationing ensured a fairer distribution of resources. Some children might not have appreciated the whale meat which was freely available because it:

> . . . tasted strongly of fish, unless you soaked it for twenty-four hours in vinegar, after which it tasted of vinegar. But there was so much of it – great big bloody steaks as big as your plate.[20]

A clear plate
means
A clear conscience

Don't take more than you can eat

Many posters offering advice on coping with rationing and shortages were produced. Do you think the message of this one is effective?

Many had never had so much meat or such a well-balanced diet before. The demand for labour during the war meant an end to unemployment, which also reduced poverty.

People accepted the wartime hardships because they saw there was little alternative. They knew that if the war was lost and Britain became part of the Nazi empire the situation would be far worse. Government inspectors (known as 'snoopers') made sure that all sections of society bore the same deprivations. It became fashionable to be shabbily dressed – Churchill set the example by frequently appearing in a simple boiler suit.

Finally, people prided themselves with 'making do', finding alternatives or substitutes for goods that were unavailable. The government produced rationed 'utility' clothes and furniture which used materials economically. Parachute silk made excellent underwear. Clumpy wooden-soled shoes came back into fashion as leather was scarce, and because stockings were unavailable many women painted their bare legs brown.

21

Women at war

In March 1941 the Minister of Labour, Ernest Bevin, said that:

> *Transfer of women from their home is one of the biggest industrial problems of the war.*[21]

In an effort to solve this problem a huge campaign to get women to take up war work voluntarily was launched. This was backed up by law, so that by 1943 all women between the ages of eighteen and fifty-one without children at home were liable for war service of one kind or another. For the first time women were conscripted.

> *By April 1943 90 per cent of all single women between the ages of 18 and 40 were in industry or the services.*[22]

Women in the armed forces belonged to the Auxiliary Territorial Service (ATS), the Women's Auxiliary Air Force (WAAF) or the

AFS
ARP   LCC

WOMEN REQUIRED FOR MOTOR DRIVING & TELEPHONIST DUTIES APPLY ANY FIRE STATION

▲ During the war, many women had the opportunity to undertake work that had previously been considered fit only for men.

◀ Members of the Women's Land Army at work in the fields planting potatoes.

Women's Royal Navy Service (WRNS). They drove vehicles, operated searchlights, aimed anti-aircraft guns (but were not allowed to fire them), and crewed harbour launches.

In industry women took jobs that were traditionally seen as men's work. Some of the jobs had always been considered too tough for women:

> *To be shut in for hours on end, with not even a window to see daylight, was grim. The noise was terrific and at night when you shut your eyes to sleep all the noise would start again in your head.* [23]

One man recalled:

> *I can remember my sister's hands – in contrast to my own – pitted with sharp metal splinters and covered in oil sores.* [23]

Other jobs were seen as highly skilled work. In September 1942 the Labour leader, Clement Attlee, reported,

> *The work the women are performing in munition factories has to be seen to be believed. Precision engineering jobs . . . are performed with dead accuracy by girls who had no industrial experience.* [24]

By the end of the war some factories were run almost entirely by women. Did women prove that they were capable of doing a 'man's' job? Compare the salaries for male and female trainee factory workers shown on page 16. Do you think a woman's labour was considered equal to a man's?

By 1943 more than 80,000 women had joined the Land Army, which was under the directorship of Lady Denman, to help with agriculture. Others joined the Auxiliary Fire Service (AFS) or the Auxiliary Nursing Service.

A one-time drama student, now in the WRNS, assisting anti-aircraft gunners in target practice. The British government recognized the invaluable contribution women could make to the war effort and used them to redress the shortage of manpower.

Most popular of all, and in many ways most successful, was the Women's Voluntary Service for Civil Defence (WVS), which had been started in 1938 by Lady Reading. Its members undertook any task asked of them, from ambulance driving to tea making. It is difficult to see how the war could have been won without the enormous contribution women made. Do you believe that the part that women played in the war changed how they were regarded by society? What do you think happened to many of the women's jobs in industry after the war, when the men they had replaced returned?

3
AIR RAID
Death from the sky

AIR RAIDS BROUGHT the full horror of war to the home front. A young girl caught in an attack remembered:

> . . . racing towards the house. E pulling me and yelling. The oddest feeling in the air all around, as if the whole air was falling apart, quite silently. And then suddenly I was on my face, just inside the kitchen door. There seemed to be waves buffeting me . . . I could hear Mrs R screaming . . . [25]

The first major attack was the Battle of Britain from July to October 1940, which was a mission to destroy the Royal Air Force. Other major raids were the Blitz, which lasted from September 1940 to May 1941; the Little Blitz from January to April 1944; and the V-1 and V-2 attacks from June 1944 to March 1945.

There were sporadic raids between these periods. The Baedeker raids from April to June 1942 were reprisal attacks made on cities of historical interest.

For most of the war the attacks came from Dornier, Junkers and Heinkel bombers which flew in huge formations protected by fighters. When daytime losses became too high the Germans turned to night attacks. Three types of bomb were used: high explosive, which buried themselves in the ground and then blew up, leaving a crater; incendiary or fire bombs; and mines, which came down on parachutes and detonated when they hit a solid object. They wrought terrible destruction on buildings. By June 1944 the Germans had introduced flying bombs – the V-1s, nicknamed doodlebugs – which were superseded by the V-2 rockets.

Britain had defences in the air and on the ground. Spitfires and Hurricanes did their

Barrage balloons reminded citizens that there was a war on, but did little to hinder high-flying bombers.

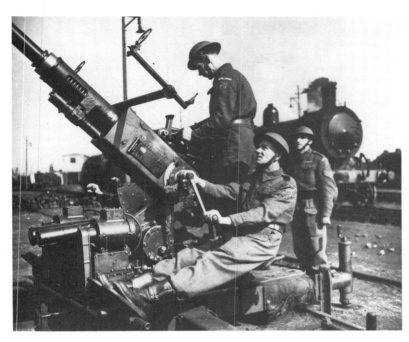

◀ An anti-aircraft gun positioned to defend a railway yard in Devonshire. It is operated by the Home Guard.

▼ A captured V-2 rocket on display in Trafalgar Square. These bombs were considered the most deadly of all because they moved faster than sound and could not be heard before they reached their target.

best to break through the screen of enemy Messerschmitt fighters and shoot down the vulnerable bombers. Radar, a British invention and still in its infancy, warned when attacks were due, enabling fighters to become airborne in time. Barrage balloons were tethered to prevent low-flying attacks from dive bombers, but they did little to stop the heavy bombers. At night the pencil beams of searchlights sought to pick up enemy aircraft, so that anti-aircraft guns firing exploding shells could get their range.

On the ground numerous measures were taken to protect the public against the bombing. Wailing sirens warned when an attack was due. Gas masks were issued to all citizens before the war because it was believed gas bombs would be dropped. Some mothers and children were evacuated to the countryside but most had returned home again by the time the serious assaults began. The ARP organized a network of fire and ambulance services, and wardens were each responsible for a street or block they knew well. Civilians used cellars, underground railway stations or special air-raid shelters to shield them from the bombs.

The children's war

Children being evacuated in 1939 to protect them from the heavy bombing that was expected to hit London and other cities when war began.

Evacuation arrangements were made before war was declared because it was generally believed that fierce bombing would begin as soon as war broke out. On 1 September 1939 there began a remarkable feat of transportation. Over one-and-a-half million women and children were evacuated from the vulnerable industrial cities and taken into the countryside. Here new homes were found for them with the inhabitants of rural towns and villages. The move was completed by the evening of 3 September. During this operation no child had been lost, injured or killed. Had evacuation been a success? Consider the following evidence and reach your own conclusion:

- Only one-third of the expected three-and-a-half million people took advantage of the voluntary evacuation scheme.
- By the summer of 1940, when the Blitz began, the majority of the evacuees had returned home. There was a second evacuation in the summer of 1940 and a third in 1944 when V-1 and V-2 attacks started.
- Many working-class children who moved into middle-class homes were amazed at what they found. Two little girls were gripped by hysterical fear when taken into

the bathroom – they had never seen a bath before and believed they were to be drowned in the tub. Other children were petrified by clean white sheets: they had never used them for sleeping in but only for laying over dead bodies.

- Hosts were horrified to find that many children were infested with fleas and lice, wet their beds and wore clothes that were in tatters.

The evacuees and their hosts quickly discovered that customs, standards and conditions in the country were markedly different to those in the inner cities. Is it possible that the enforced intermingling of town and country, rich and poor, could have had unforeseen benefits?

For most children the war was a strange mixture of boredom and excitement.

> *For most of the time life just went on as normal – well, it wasn't really normal because we had to go without so many things; Mum was at work all the time, and Dad was away. It was quite boring really. Then something amazing would happen, like a German bomber being shot down in a field near our house, or news of D-Day.* [26]

If the war was boring for some British children, it was hardly so for the Germans when Allied armies invaded their country in December 1944. Some of the captured German soldiers were only fourteen. Do you think it was right to call up boys of that age, even in an emergency?

▲ Young German boys who had joined the army in 1944 when more troops were recruited in a desperate attempt to drive back the Allies.

▶ Evacuees enjoying themselves in the countryside. Being away from home was clearly not all misery and provided new experiences for many city children.

The Blitz

'The Blitz' was a popular phrase for the German bombing raids on the British cities in 1940 and 1941. The term came from the German word 'blitzkrieg', meaning 'lightning war', the tactic of combining aircraft and armoured divisions in rapid, devastating attacks. Because no land forces were involved, the air raids on Britain were not really blitzkrieg at all.

The purpose of the German raids was twofold. Firstly, to damage Britain's war effort, by destroying factories, oil depots and other key installations. Secondly, to break people's morale, softening them up for invasion, or forcing them to sue for peace. Why did neither of these aims succeed?

On the night of 14/15 November 1940 the Germans made one of their heaviest raids of the war on the city of Coventry. The next day a newspaper reported:

> *Coventry has been the victim of the most concentrated, if not the worst, raid since the war began. I have just come back from the centre of the city, which now looks exactly like one of those French towns that were laid level during the last war by an intensive bombardment.*
>
> *The cathedral is in ruins, except for its tower, and over a large area surrounding it there lies the stench of burning houses.*[27]

This cartoon by Low, from the *Evening Standard*, 11 September, 1940, depicts Reich Marshal Hermann Goering dropping bombs on 'the Cockney Heart'.

Such devastation might be expected to dishearten the inhabitants of the city. But the reporter goes on to say:

> *This is not a mortal blow to our war production by any means, and I should not be surprised if quite soon work is resumed in Coventry to some extent.*
>
> *In every heart there is not fear, only a most passionate hatred of the enemy, and a determination to carry on at all costs.*[27]

Did the German policy of aerial bombardment fail because it was not heavy enough to damage the war effort seriously, although it destroyed 86,000 homes and killed 60,595 civilians? The evidence suggests that it only made people more determined not to give in. Instead of breaking morale, it appeared to raise it. When the Allies bombed German cities they found the same thing. British and American raids on Germany were far heavier – over 1,000 four-engined bombers dropped thousands of tonnes of bombs in a single day – but German factories still continued their production. It seems that it was only with the invention of the atomic bomb, which could destroy a whole city at the flick of a switch, that bombing became decisive in the outcome of war.

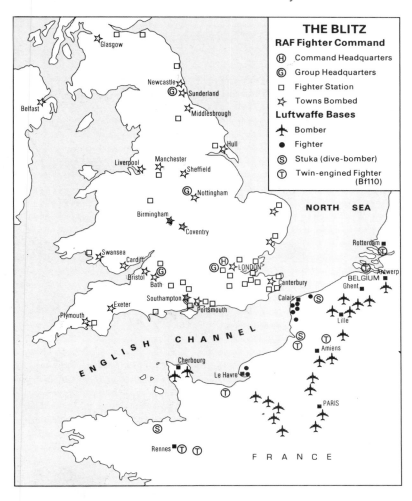

A map of Britain showing where the Germans concentrated their bombing raids in the summer of 1940.

Counter-attack

◀ An American B17 bomber, known as the 'Flying Fortress'. Note the gun turrets.

▼ Thousands of German families were made homeless by Allied bombing and were forced to wander the streets with their belongings, looking for shelter.

Consider this extract from the diary of the German Propaganda Minister, Joseph Goebbels:

> *May 16, 1943. The day raids by American bombers are creating extraordinary difficulties. . . . serious damage to military and technical installations of the navy . . . If this continues we shall have to face serious consequences which in the long run will prove unbearable.*
> *May 25. The night raid of the English on Dortmund was extraordinarily heavy, probably the worst ever directed against a German city . . . Industrial and munition plants have been hit very hard . . . The people in the west are beginning to lose courage . . .*[28]

This is the opinion of one man. He believed that the bombing raids were having two effects. Firstly, they were destroying German factories, making it more difficult for them to manufacture armaments. How might a historian check Goebbels' belief to see if it was true? The second effect of the bombing, according to Propaganda Minister Goebbels, was to weaken German morale.

The American historian W. L. Shirer accepts what Goebbels said:

> *The greatest damage inflicted by the Anglo-American air forces, as Goebbels makes clear in his diary, was to the homes and morale of the German people . . . it is not surprising that as 1943 approached its end . . . the German people began to despair and realize that this was the beginning of the end . . .*[29]

Yet the British historian A. J. P. Taylor disagrees:

> *Many thousands of Germans were killed, and tens of thousands were made homeless . . . Certainly the German standard of life was reduced for the first time, though it never fell to the British level. But morale was unaffected.*[30]

The effect of Allied bombing is an important and controversial topic in the history of the Second World War. Do these statistics suggest that bombing seriously cut back German production?

The 'weapons of war' were heavy guns, tanks and aircraft. But these figures do not tell the whole story. They do not mention, for example, the quality of the weapons produced or the supplies of fuel available to operate them.

Morale is even more difficult to measure. If the Germans were really 'beginning to lose courage' in 1943 as Goebbels believed, would you have expected them to have gone on fighting right up until the moment when Russian troops occupied Berlin two years later? Or were the Allied forces able to advance into Germany *because* their enemy's morale was low? Can you think of any other signs of low German morale in 1944–5?

Year	Tonnes of bombs dropped by the Allies	Numbers of German weapons of war produced
1942	48,000	36,804
1944	915,000	105,258 [30]

A map showing the principal targets of Allied bombers. The Ruhr was a major industrial area, and the centre of steel production. Almost unbelievably, German industrial production rose steadily until 1945, despite the heavy bomb attacks.

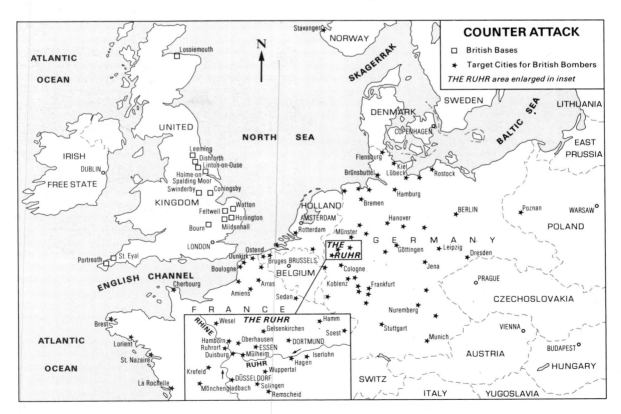

31

4

MORALE
Propaganda and pleasure

IN NOVEMBER 1939 a young French soldier in the front line wrote in his diary:

> *We're all getting bored and our morale is declining. Several of my comrades who left their families without support are wondering what they're doing here. This is a war of words and not of battles. Radio Stuttgart often broadcasts messages in French. A voice tells us that we fought enough in the First War . . . and . . . the Führer only wants one thing and that is peace.*[31]

In war the morale of the fighting forces and the civilians is as important as military strength. A weaker force can defeat a stronger one if it believes it can win, if it has confidence in itself. Do you think that the extract above indicates why the French armies collapsed so rapidly in the face of the German assault in the spring and early summer of 1940?

At the start of the war the Germans understood better than anyone else the importance of maintaining the morale of their own people and lowering that of the enemy. Their citizens and soldiers were allowed to hear nothing but messages of victory. Massive parades, skilfully-worded articles and clever films all helped to make the Germans believe they were invincible.

The British were slow to realize the importance of morale. Many early statements by the Ministry of Information were tactless and were mocked by the people, who called it the 'Mystery of Information'. However, the war might have been lost if morale on the home front had not been high in general. The

Oxford crowds queuing to see a Laurel and Hardy film, October 1940. A visit to the cinema was a popular way of forgetting the war for a few hours.

This poster, telling people they can help win the war by investing in government War Savings, is also a form of anti-Nazi propaganda. The Nazi 'bug' is part insect, part devil.

government developed all kinds of ways to get the British people to believe that they could win. There were poster campaigns, edited news broadcasts and propaganda films. The newspapers helped too. But most influential were the stirring speeches of Winston Churchill.

Despite the restrictions resulting from the war, the government also did what it could to enable citizens to enjoy themselves. It organized and encouraged concerts and comedy shows on stage and on the radio.

Although theatres and cinemas were closed down when war first broke out, the authorities soon realized their mistake and allowed them to reopen. London's Windmill Theatre proudly proclaimed that it never closed, and shows put on there and in other places of entertainment brought pleasure to thousands. The British managed to keep their sense of humour and their cheerfulness. This was important for morale and enabled most of them to come through the horrors of war still smiling.

We will never surrender

RECEPTION COMMITTEE

By early 1940 British discontent with the government's handling of the war was widespread. The previous September many people had expected the war to be over by Christmas. The firmly held belief was that 'the bomber would always get through.'[32] Either Germany or Britain and its allies would be pounded to defeat within weeks. One woman recalls hearing, and believing, a rumour that on the evening of 3 September – the very day that war broke out – the whole of London was in flames.[33] In fact, apart from some naval battles, nothing happened for months. The only taste of war the British were given was deprivation and government ineffectuality.

Hitler declared he would force Britain to surrender by 15 August 1940. What is this cartoon's message?

The British were ready for the sacrifices of a war which had been predicted for months, if not years. They were prepared to accept rationing, black-out, conscription and evacuation as long as there seemed a point to it. But they felt starved of information.

Censorship seemed idiotic; millions of leaflets (why not bombs?) were dropped on Germany, but the British press were not told their contents in case they revealed information 'which might be of some use to the enemy'. Men smoking their pipes while walking home from the pub were reprimanded for breaking the black-out. This was not the sort of war people had been led to expect. How would you describe the following speaker's attitude?

> We're sure to win the war ... when Hitler dies of old age and the German people take pity on us.[34]

Perhaps a million people listened to the German propaganda of William Joyce, nicknamed Lord Haw-Haw for his adopted upper-class accent. His radio broadcasts were designed to undermine British self-confidence and created a rash of rumours and scares.

Then in April 1940 came the sudden collapse of Denmark. On 10 May the Germans swept into Holland, France and Belgium, and Chamberlain tendered his resignation the same day. Chamberlain had told the British people that there would be no war; his heart had not been in the conflict. Why do you think that he felt it necessary to resign?

Soon there came news of terrible defeats, and by the end of the summer the Blitz had begun. This was the kind of war the British had been anticipating. Churchill, the new prime minister, made a rousing speech. Can you imagine the effect this had on morale?

> ... we shall defend our island, whatever the cost may be, we shall fight on the beaches, we shall fight on the landing grounds, we shall fight in the fields and in the streets, we shall fight in the hills; we shall never surrender.[35]

Had Churchill understood the mood of the British at this time?

An ENSA concert in a munitions factory. The government supported ENSA's efforts to provide light entertainment for troops and factory workers.

Keep smiling

Strangely, one of the mistakes made by the Chamberlain government was to approach the task of communicating with the people in too serious a manner. Much of the work of the Ministry of Information was well-meaning, earnest – but dull. People felt that they were being talked down to. Important information may be better received if it is presented in a lively or humorous way.

Throughout the war the government kept up a campaign urging citizens not to gossip idly about the war, for fear that they might reveal vital information to enemy spies or damage morale. Here are two ways in which the problem was tackled. Which do you think is more effective?

1. Government announcement:

Do you know Mr Secrecy Hugh Hush, Mr Knowall, Miss Leaky Mouth, Miss Teacup Whisper, Mr Pride in Prophecy, Mr Glumpot? Tell these people to JOIN BRITAIN'S SILENT COLUMN, the great body of sensible men and women who have pledged themselves not to talk rumour and gossip and stop others doing it.[36]

2. Study carefully the portrait behind the two speakers in the Fougasse cartoon on page 37.

When the war broke out the government closed all theatres and cinemas, and limited the BBC radio (known as wireless) to one programme. Television broadcasts, which were in their infancy, had been shut down just before war was declared. Before long it was realized that such austerity did little for morale. A harassed and anxious people needed to relax.

The BBC provided the key link between the government and the people. Services were carefully controlled. In an effort to combat

Tommy Handley and two of the cast of ITMA ('It's That Man Again'). This popular radio comedy programme probably did more than any of the government propaganda to raise the morale of the British people.

"....strictly between these four walls!"

CARELESS TALK COSTS LIVES

This Fougasse cartoon was one in a series of posters using humour to put across a serious message.

rumours and prevent panic, it became the Ministry of Information's policy to allow the public as much information as was safe to give them. Almost every off-duty person in the country listened to the Nine O'Clock News, while lighter programmes, such as Tommy Handley's comedy programme ITMA ('It's That Man Again') and Music While You Work provided entertainment and helped keep up morale.

ENSA organized concerts and other entertainments all over the country in the most unlikely places. Films, such as Noël Coward's famous *In Which We Serve*, combined pleasure with propaganda, as did popular songs. 'There'll Always Be An England' became almost an alternative national anthem. Vera Lynn was a popular figure at this time and her songs were frequently played over the radio. What contribution do you think entertainments made to the war effort?

5
THE ENEMY WITHIN
The secret war

WITHIN BRITAIN DURING the war there were three categories of suspicious foreigner: spies (when they could be discovered), aliens and prisoners of war. There was a great deal of talk about spies and spying, but few German agents were captured and they appear never to have been a real threat.

'Aliens' were divided into three categories. Class A were those who openly proclaimed their pro-Nazi sympathies. They were arrested as soon as hostilities were declared and interned for the rest of the war. Those who had only just arrived in Britain were placed in Class B. About 60,000 refugees had flooded into Britain by September 1939, fleeing from Nazi tyranny. At first they were just restricted – they were not allowed to own a car, for example. But in May 1940, when the Germans smashed through the western defences, all Class B aliens who had German connections were locked up. Class C, the largest group, comprised all refugees and Germans who had lived in Britain for at least six years. At first they were treated well, but in 1940 many of them joined the other classes in internment camps. The government was taking no chances. Nazis, anti-Nazis, Jews and even Jew-baiters were thus all imprisoned together.

Jewish refugees arriving in Britain from Germany in 1939. A year later many of them were interned as a possible security risk.

In May 1940 many foreigners were rounded up and sent under military escort to internment camps where they often encountered unpleasant, overcrowded conditions.

Often the conditions in the camps were below the standard of military prisoner of war camps because they were intended to be used temporarily. Many people were shocked at the treatment of internees when the facts came to light.

By the end of 1940 about 1,000 German and Italian prisoners of war were held in Britain. They were quite well looked after, and the Italians became popular with the local population. Unlike their British counterparts in Germany, not one enemy prisoner managed to escape. At first the Germans were so confident that Germany would soon invade Britain that not many even attempted to escape.

Throughout the war Germany held thousands of Allied prisoners. Although they were continually trying to escape, the British did not suffer undue hardships. Members of other nations fared far worse, as did opponents of the Nazi regime and members of the European resistance movements held by the Nazis. They often found themselves in concentration camps where they were treated most brutally. The worst fate was reserved for Jews, gypsies and other minority groups who were systematically exterminated in death camps from 1942 onwards.

Throughout occupied Europe there operated an effective network of spies and a vigorous resistance movement. Some of their work was passive, such as handing on vital information to London. They also assisted prisoners to escape and damaged the German war effort with sabotage.

Prisoners

German prisoners taking exercise in a Scottish prisoner of war camp. Why do you think prisoners of war found it more difficult to escape from Britain than from Nazi Germany?

During the Second World War the British did not display the extreme hatred of the enemy that there had been in the First World War. A subtle distinction was generally made between 'Germans' and 'Nazis'. Most Germans, it was felt, had been led astray by a handful of vicious politicians.

Prisoners of war were kept in makeshift camps, made from converted hotels, country houses or other suitably remote large buildings. They wore blue dungarees marked with large patches or jackets with 'PW' on them to identify them as prisoners. Much of the prisoners' time was spent idly sitting around, playing games, plotting to escape or just dreaming of home.

Many prisoners also had the opportunity to work. After all, during the war Britain was faced with a labour shortage and it seemed only sensible for the government to use all available able-bodied men. Many of the tasks that prisoners undertook were manual – rebuilding roads or helping on farms – but some POWs were entrusted with more skilled jobs, such as making maps. All working prisoners received a few shillings a week in wages. Several farmers were most impressed with the efficiency shown by the Germans – one farmer's wife even gave them extra food as a way of saying thank you.[37]

One *Luftwaffe* pilot remembered how he had been treated when captured during the Battle of Britain:

> When my plane was hit I bailed out, a bullet crease along my scalp, blood running into my eyes. But I came down safely, and the Home Guard was there to meet me. They were unfailingly kind.[38]

Did the fact that there were thousands of British captives in German POW camps perhaps affect the way the British treated their German prisoners?

Many more POWs escaped from Germany than from Britain. When considering why this was so, the following points ought to be borne in mind:

1. The difficulty of escape from Britain, as it involved travel by boat or plane.
2. The existence in Europe of a number of neutral countries, such as Sweden or Switzerland, which sheltered escapees.
3. The relatively friendly treatment of German POWs in Britain.
4. There were many thousands of British POWs, compared with the few German ones in Britain, and many Germans were later taken to countries in the British Empire (such as Canada) from where escape was virtually impossible.
5. The possibility that German morale was falling after 1942.
6. The help given to British escapees from friendly organizations in occupied lands.

German prisoners of war cleaning a London street. Due to the labour shortage, many of the prisoners were employed in manual tasks for which they were paid a small wage.

Resistance

'Resistance' is the word used to describe the efforts of men and women within Germany and occupied Europe who fought on their home front against Nazi domination. Because of the stranglehold of the secret police, resistance within Germany was very limited. Its most famous exploit was the Bomb Plot of 20 July 1944, when an attempt was made to kill Hitler in his 'Wolf's Lair' headquarters in East Prussia. A bomb exploded beneath the table at which the Führer was sitting, causing enormous damage but failing to kill its intended victim. The conspirators were rounded up and, after a farce of a trial, were hanged.

Outside Germany resistance took many forms. A good deal of work was done to help Britain and the USA gather information by supplying them with pictures, maps and data on matters such as troop movements.

Another tactic was to give the Germans misinformation – false reports on what was going on. The resistance also spread anti-Nazi propaganda, helping to undermine the oppressive regime from within. Scores of British escapees were aided by the resistance network as they made their way across Europe to the safety of a neutral country.

The most dramatic action undertaken by the resistance was armed attack or sabotage on German military targets. This might involve assassinations, destroying communications or simply removing vital pieces from weapons in an armaments factory. Such acts did not have a dramatic effect on the course of the war, but they did help. One problem

Hitler examining the room damaged by the explosion when a bomb attempt was made on his life in July 1944.

Members of the French Resistance helping American soldiers, August 1944. By this time the Allies had landed in Normandy and had begun to push the German Army eastward.

was that Nazi reprisals for acts of resistance could be terrible. In 1942 three Czech agents assassinated the Nazi leader Reinhard Heydrich. The Germans executed everyone they could lay their hands on with the same surnames as the assassins, and wiped out the villages of Lidice and Lezaky. Over 2,000 people were killed as a reprisal for the death of one man.

How effective was the resistance? Consider this statement by an historian of the movement :

André Gillois has recorded that General de Gaulle said to me one day, 'Between you and me, Resistance was a bluff that came off.' There is an element of truth in this: resistance's real strength in battlefield terms, in an age of armour and air warfare, was puny. But it had titanic, as it turned out invincible, strength in moral terms. It gave back to people in the occupied countries the self-respect they had lost in the moment of occupation.[39]

General Charles de Gaulle, the commander of the Free French in Britain, inspecting one of his commando units.

Spies

A Tyneside man remembered his attitude to government warnings about spies:

His Majesty's Government, in their wisdom, had told us that 'Walls have ears' and 'Look out – there's a spy about'. Wall posters – by far the most fascinating to me was the Spy poster. Depicted was a city gent in bowler, with brolly, striped trousers, black coat and carrying a briefcase. This person, we were confidentially informed, could be a spy.[40]

Why was he fascinated by the Spy poster? Do you think posters like these would have made people more careful in their conversation?

In fact Britain was a very difficult country to spy on during the Second World War because everyone was highly suspicious of strangers and the island's isolation made new arrivals stand out. A Newcastle Civil Servant was reported to the police for writing postcards in a remote Northumberland village – the villagers thought that she was sketching the area in order to make a map for the Germans!

▲ This Ministry of Information poster was part of a huge anti-gossip campaign. It was considered vitally important not to let information fall into enemy hands.

◄ The punishment for spying in occupied Europe could be very harsh as the execution of these partisans in the Balkans shows.

The government had to be cautious in using information gathered from German coded messages. Coventry was left largely undefended when it was known that a major air raid was planned. Could the devastation that ensued have been avoided?

Spies who did arrive were surprisingly poorly prepared for their work. They carried oversized radio transmitters in bulky suitcases. One showed his ignorance of British customs by trying to order a drink in a pub at nine in the morning. Others left foreign labels in their clothes, replied 'Ja' to questions when not thinking, or wrote continental sevens (7). It is even said that a spy arrived in Britain carrying a half-eaten German sausage. Perhaps he was hoping that no one could possibly suspect someone who was so obviously German? No Allied operation was endangered by information gathered by a German spy operating in Britain. The home front turned out to be spy-proof, but given the number of foreign refugees who had come to Britain do you think the warnings against spies were totally unjustified?

Agents operating in occupied Europe were more successful. With so many people of different nationalities – refugees, workers and prisoners – moving around the continent it was of course much more difficult for the Germans to operate an effective counter-espionage system. It was possible, for example, for the British to give Stalin ample warning of the 'surprise' German attack on Soviet Russia in June 1941.

The most remarkable piece of Allied information gathering did not involve spies at all, but a machine known as 'Ultra'. This enabled Churchill to read almost all top secret German messages put out in their 'Enigma' code. The information was invaluable. Yet the government did not dare to act upon everything they discovered, lest the Germans grew suspicious. Might this be one reason why Churchill left Coventry undefended when he knew that the Germans intended to raid the city?

Home Guard

This humorous portrayal of the Home Guard by Emett in *Punch* was in fact very close to the truth in many parts of Britain.

" I grant you it MIGHT be a bit awkward if the invasion came up Cherry Lane instead of the High Street."

On Tuesday 14 May 1940 the Secretary of State for War, Anthony Eden, appealed for volunteers to join the new Local Defence Volunteers. A quarter of a million men joined within the first twenty-four hours. By July the force numbered over a million. It was a genuine response to the need to resist invasion by those unable to join the regular forces through age or because they were needed elsewhere. There is no doubting their enthusiasm, but how effective would the force really have been in the face of German paratroopers or regular units charging up the beaches?

Compare the two views of the Home Guard – as the force came to be known – which are expressed in the official recruitment poster on page 47 and the cartoon from *Punch* shown above. What impression of the Home Guard does the government poster try to create? How, on the contrary, does the cartoon characterize members of the Home Guard? Which, if either, do you suppose was nearer the truth?

The initial weakness of the Home Guard was that it lacked professional training and modern weaponry. At best men carried old-fashioned rifles. Others made do with shotguns, or even pikes made of bayonets on metal poles. How useful would these have been against an invading Panzer division? Uniforms were ill-fitting, giving the Guard a ridiculous look, and elected officers frequently had their authority questioned.

On the other hand, units of the Home Guard had local knowledge and determination. They prepared ambushes in places they knew well. All possible glider landing grounds were blocked off. In the last resort, as Churchill defiantly announced, they could always take a German with them – meaning that each man could kill a German if he were prepared to commit suicide in the process. The Home Guard had an élite force, the 'Auxiliary Unit', who were hand-picked for their skill, knowledge, ruthlessness and imagination. Their task was to lie low if the Germans invaded, then re-emerge behind enemy lines and wage guerrilla warfare. They were trained in sabotage and hand-to-hand fighting.

The part-time Home Guard was disbanded in the winter of 1944. The threat of invasion had long since passed and Guard members had developed into a force of anti-aircraft gunners and assistants to the regular forces. By this time the Home Guard was much better trained and equipped and had come a long way from its disorganized beginnings. Do you think it had a useful contribution to make or was it just 'playing at soldiers'?

▲ A Home Guard recruitment poster. In reality, the men were rarely as well equipped as the one in the picture.

◀ Home Guard soldiers training with anti-tank guns.

6
A NATION'S VICTORY
The Yanks

THE USA ENTERED the war in December 1941. The first American soldiers and airmen arrived in Britain in 1942. Over the next three years they were followed by several million more, on their way to the battlefields of Europe or stationed on American air bases. One historian has written of them:

> *The American invasion struck the British Isles like a huge technicolor bomb, scattering nylons, cigarettes and candy and goodwill over the whole country.*[41]

The war-battered British were amazed at their allies, who seemed so rich, so open and friendly, so confident.

American service personnel were paid five times as much as their British counterparts. Moreover, their government ensured that they were kept supplied with most of the home luxuries which had not been seen in Britain for years: chewing gum, nylon stockings ('nylons'), oranges, plentiful butter and spirits. To the women of Britain, many of whose husbands and boyfriends were away

American GIs socializing with British ATS girls. British men often resented the wealth and popularity of their American Allies.

Three sisters, whose father had been killed in an air raid, are treated to a visit to the cinema. Orphaned British children, selected by the American Red Cross, were 'adopted' by US Army engineers who provided extra financial assistance. Such acts of kindness won the Americans many friends.

on active service, they seemed like an army of film stars. Relationships flourished between American soldiers (known as GIs because their kit was marked 'Government Issue') and British girls. Some were casual: the incidence of sexually transmitted diseases soared, as did the number of illegitimate births. Some were serious: thousands of British girls became 'GI brides', leaving home after the war to start a new life in the USA.

The GIs had a somewhat different effect on British servicemen. A popular phrase was that the transatlantic allies were, 'Overpaid, oversexed – and over here'. One British soldier returning unexpectedly to find his wife with an American airman threw the unfortunate flyer from a second floor window. An RAF fitter gives his reaction to the American invasion:

Bloody Yanks! They came into the war late, when we had been bled white. Then they swanked about with all their money, thinking that they could buy anything. Even our women.[42]

What different effects do you think the GIs had on home front morale?

Most people in Britain found the GIs unfailingly generous and helpful; for example, damage caused by their military vehicles was repaired at once, and the Christmas parties they gave for British children were legendary. But there was one aspect of American culture the British found difficult to admire or accept – racism. Segregation still existed in the southern USA, and bullying, prejudice and even fighting seemed sadly inappropriate among men fighting on the same side.

Five years on

The Second World War ended in Europe at midnight on 8 May 1945. The sense of relief was overwhelming but tempered by several restraining factors. In the Far East the fighting against Japan still went on. As the hostilities ceased the full horror of the Nazi regime became widely known – the death camps, torture and unbelievable cruelty. In Britain there was time to mourn the dead and count the cost of the damage. Gradually a powerful sense of anticlimax came over the nation.

The war left Britain's economy in turmoil. There were to be more years of rationing after the war than during it. In one of the greatest shocks, at least as far as foreign correspondents were concerned, Churchill's Conservative Party was overwhelmingly defeated in the general election of 5 July. Great war leader he might have been, but the electorate now wanted to see the building of a new, fairer Britain.

A VE Day street party, May 1945. Celebrations took place all over the country as the British rejoiced in the fact that, after long years of hardship and deprivation, the war had finally ended.

Moving in, 1945. Thousands of prefabricated houses were manufactured for families bombed out of their own homes as an immediate, though temporary, solution to the housing shortage.

poverty that existed in some areas, and reforms had been discussed. The Beveridge Report of 1942 advocated a social security and national health system. The Education Act of 1944 made provision for some form of secondary education for every child. Consider the chief changes made by the government. Do you think that they were a continuation of the policies employed on the home front from 1939 to 1945?

- Establishment of the National Health Service.
- Nationalization of the coal, iron and steel, gas and electricity industries.
- Nationalization of railways and inland waterways.
- School leaving age raised. Free school milk issued.
- Town and Country Planning Act introduced radical measures to protect the countryside and provide new housing.

During the Second World War the British people worked together in a manner unprecedented in their history. Those who lived on the home front never forgot the sense of unity and co-operation which the Nazi threat brought. We might ask ourselves nowadays, when there is no external danger, how that spirit could be recaptured.

The Labour government that came to power in the summer of 1945 introduced a social revolution: the Welfare State. The war had made the government aware of the

A scene during the general election of 1945. The figures for the parties' gains and losses indicate the mood of the voters.

Leading figures

Beaverbrook, Lord (W. M. Aitken) (1879–1964) member of the war cabinet 1940–42

William Maxwell Aitken made a fortune in Canada before emigrating to Britain in 1910. He made a successful entry into politics, acquiring the title Lord Beaverbrook in 1917 and becoming Minister of Information in 1918. Between the wars he built up a newspaper empire (*Daily Express*, *Sunday Express* and *Evening Standard*). Always a close friend of Winston Churchill, he was made Minister of Aircraft Production in May 1940. To this crucial post he brought his great dynamism, doubling the production of aircraft in three months. The same energy infected the Ministry of Supply when he took it over a year later. He remained a key figure in Churchill's wartime administration, close to the premier, respected for his energy, mistrusted for his prejudices.

Bevin, Ernest (1881–1951) Minister of Labour 1940–45

From humble beginnings as a farm labourer Ernest Bevin worked his way to the top of the trade union movement. He was largely responsible for the creation of the Transport and General Workers' Union and became Chairman of the TUC in 1937. When Churchill formed his coalition cabinet in May 1940 Bevin was his obvious choice as Minister of Labour. He entered the war cabinet a few months later. His working-class background and his union connections were invaluable in helping him fulfil his duties. He was responsible for directing all the nation's labour, shocking many by sending conscripts down the coal mines and conscripting middle-aged women. Bevin's partnership with Churchill symbolized the wartime unity of the nation.

Churchill, Winston L. S. (1874–1965) prime minister 1940–45

By the mid-1930s it looked as if Churchill's political career was at an end. He was in his sixties and appeared to be out of touch with public opinion, opposing his party over its policy towards Indian nationalism and appeasement of the Nazis. On this latter issue, however, he was proved right and when Chamberlain resigned in May 1940 Churchill was chosen to become prime minister. His wide experience as soldier, journalist and cabinet minister fitted him well to the task. He also possessed the right blend of aristocratic confidence and theatrical doggedness (cigar and V-sign), coupled with considerable talents as an orator, to enable him to win and hold the people's trust and affection. Although possessed of many faults, not least of which was a belief that he knew best how to do everybody's job, he more than anyone else held the British people together during the difficult times of 1940–42.

de Gaulle, Charles A. J. M. (1890–1970) 'Free French' leader 1940–45

An imposing figure with a distinct profile, Charles de Gaulle was responsible for upholding French honour during the bitter years of Nazi occupation, 1940–44. He trained as a soldier, was wounded in the First World War, and became one of the first officers in France to understand the importance of the tank in modern warfare. He fought with considerable skill in 1940, held a government post for a few days, then fled to England. Here he saw it as his duty to rally his country and resist the conscious or unconscious efforts of the Allies to belittle its status. This led him into several rows with Churchill (he was in a way a French version of Churchill) and the Americans, but ensured that when he returned to his native land in 1944 he was hailed as a national hero.

Denman, Lady G. M. (1884–1954) director of the Women's Land Army 1939–45

From a wealthy, privileged background, Gertrude Mary Denman enjoyed a fine career as a public servant. She first made her name as chairwoman of the National Federation of Women's Institutes, a post she held until 1946. In the 1930s she led the National Birth Control Association. Lady Denman believed strongly in the rights and abilities of women. She was appointed director of the Women's Land Army in 1939. She found the work of the organization hampered by male prejudice and ministerial inefficiency, against which she successfully employed her administrative skills and driving energy.

Goebbels, Joseph P. (1887–1945) German Propaganda Minister 1933–45

In many ways Goebbels was responsible for the creation of the popularity of Hitler and the Nazi Party. Lameness caused his rejection by the army during the Great War and produced a deep personal bitterness. He gave vent to this by studying how the masses could be manipulated by censorship and propaganda, and by developing a belief in fanatical ruthlessness. In 1933 Hitler appointed him Minister of Enlightenment and Propaganda. Goebbels used this post to feed the German people with half-truths and vivid images to build up their belief in themselves and their Führer. He also attempted to make them hate all opponents of the Third Reich. Responsible for the concept of 'total war' in 1943, Goebbels killed his family and himself in 1945 rather than face capture.

Joseph Goebbels, the Nazi Propaganda Minister who brilliantly exploited the mass media to build up a favourable image for his party.

Handley, Tommy R. (1892–1949) radio comedian

Tommy Handley was the man who made the nation laugh during the difficult years of war. He also started a style of British humour which lived on in the Goon Show and Monty Python. Liverpool born, Handley first made a name for himself as a stage comedian. When wireless (radio) became common in the 1920s he embraced the new medium with enthusiasm. From 1939 to 1949 he was the star and inspiration behind the immensely popular weekly comedy programme of daily life, ITMA – standing for 'It's That Man Again'. The programmes were full of wit and sparkle, poking gentle fun at the British way of life through Mrs Mopp the cleaner, the Office of Twerps (a typical bungling ministry), and Foaming-at-the-Mouth, a seaside resort. Tommy Handley did as much as anyone to maintain morale on the home front during the war years.

Joyce, William (1906–46) propagandist

During the first six months of the war hundreds of thousands of British citizens listened with some interest to the broadcasts made in English from Germany. The most popular ones were the work of William Joyce, an Irish-American fascist who had fled from Britain to Germany with his second wife in 1939. He adopted an easily-mimicked English upper-class drawl, which earned him the nickname 'Lord Haw-Haw' and stood out in his opening announcement: 'Jairmany calling'. He mocked British life with a number of stock figures such as the parson with shares in the armaments industry, 'good old bumbly Mannering', or the Jewish tax evader, Sir Izzy Ungeheimer. At a time when the nation was unsure what the war was about, Haw-Haw's stories of the good life in Germany and the foolishness of the British to be fighting caused some concern. But his audiences fell away when the war became horribly real in the summer of 1940. He was hung for treason in 1946.

Lynn, Dame Vera (1917–) singer

For many in the British armed forces the overriding problem of the war was not danger so much as boredom and a sense of isolation from families and loved ones. The singer Vera Lynn played an important part cheering the lives of these lonely people. She had her own programme ('Sincerely Yours') and travelled widely to sing to troops stationed in different parts of the globe. She also made several films. At first the government did not approve of her way of lifting morale, calling her singing 'slush', and they wanted to replace it with military marches. But with songs such as 'Some Sunny Day' (usually known as 'We'll Meet Again') and 'The White Cliffs of Dover' she earned the title of 'The Sweetheart of the Forces', and the undying affection of the nation.

Vera Lynn, the 'Forces' Sweetheart', one of the best-known entertainers of the war years.

Lady Reading, who founded the Women's Voluntary Service.

Morrison, Herbert S. (1888–1965) member of Churchill's government

Herbert Morrison rose to prominence through the Labour Party, starting in local politics then becoming an MP and sitting on the London County Council. Churchill recognized Morrison's talent at once and made him Minister of Supply in May 1940. His watchword 'Go to it' caught the popular imagination and output was stepped up considerably under his forceful direction. From October 1940 to the end of the war he served as Home Secretary, with a seat in the cabinet from 1942. He was responsible for civil defence, created the National Fire Service and kept an overall eye on censorship. He gave his name to a type of bomb shelter which fitted inside people's houses: it was like a huge steel table with tough wire mesh at the sides. Over a million were in use by the end of the war.

Reading, Lady Stella (1894–1971) organizer of the WVS

The threat of war in 1938 led Lady Reading to form the Women's Voluntary Services for Civil Defence (WVS) starting with five names selected from her address book. The movement grew rapidly, so when hostilities broke out the next year it was able to play a very significant part in the war effort. Her aim was to provide an organization which every woman could join and which would undertake any task, no matter how small. She led the way with her personal example, even going down on hands and knees to scrub steps when required to do so. Her appeal in 1940 to the housewives of the nation for aluminium with which to make aeroplanes had an overwhelming response. Through the efforts of people such as Lady Reading, the home front made an invaluable contribution to the war.

Important dates

(References are to Britain unless stated otherwise.)

Date   **Events**

1933   Hitler comes to power in Germany.

1936   Germans move troops into the Rhineland.

March Germany annexes Austria.

June RAF recruitment drive.

September Czechoslovakia agrees to the Anglo-French plan to surrender the Sudetenland to Germany; Prime Minister Chamberlain promises 'Peace for our time'.

December 'National Register' proposed, organizing all citizens in case of war; massive air-raid shelter building programme.

1939   *March* Germans occupy Czechoslovakian Bohemia.

April Britain promises to defend Poland, Romania and Greece.

June Conscription begins.

July Women's Auxiliary Air Force established.

August Emergency war powers granted to the government; reserves called up; fleet mobilized.

September War declared; many women and children evacuated from cities; income tax up to 37½p in the pound; British troops begin to land in France.

October Food prices controlled by law; unused land to be ploughed up.

1940   *January* Food rationing introduced.

March Meat rationing introduced; first civilian killed in air raid.

April Germans invade Denmark; Purchase Tax introduced.

May Germans sweep into Holland, Belgium, France and Luxemburg; Churchill becomes prime minister; Lord Beaverbrook becomes Minister of Aircraft Production; British forces retreat to Dunkirk; Emergency Powers (Defence) Act; Local Defence Volunteers (Home Guard) formed.

July 24 per cent tax on luxuries; Battle of Britain begins.

August First German bombing raid on London.

September Blitz on London begins; Battle of the Atlantic begins.

November 568 civilians killed in raid on Coventry.

1941   *April* Income tax to 50 per cent; 500 planes raid London.

May House of Commons bombed; food supplies arrive from the USA.

June Clothes and coal rationed.

December USA enters war; call-up for single women aged between twenty and thirty.

1942   *January* Churchill wins major vote of censure in the House of Commons; first US troops arrive.

March White bread banned; utility clothes introduced.

July Sweet rationing introduced; Churchill wins another vote of censure.

October Milk ration cut.

December Beveridge Report plans for the Welfare State.

1943   *January* USAF makes first daylight raids on Germany.

April 100 per cent tax on luxuries; 'Blockbuster' bombs dropped on Germany as part of massive raids.

May 'Dam Buster' raid; call-up for women aged between eighteen and forty-five.

Date	Events
	July Hamburg heavily bombed.
	October Dock strike.
	December Young conscripts ordered into coal mines.
1944	*January* Large numbers of American GIs arrive in London.
	March Coal miners' strike.
	June D-Day; V-1 flying bombs hit England.
	July Children evacuated from the path of the V-1s.
	September V-2 rockets hit southern England; black-out partially lifted.
	November Home Guard stood down.
1945	*February* Dresden devastated by Allied bombing raid.
	May Germany surrenders – VE Day.
	June Parliament dissolved after nine-and-a-half years.
	July Labour win general election.
	August Atomic bombs dropped on Hiroshima and Nagasaki; Japan surrenders.
	September VJ Day; press censorship lifted.
	October Dock strike; severe austerity; shortages remain.
1946	Wartime rations re-introduced and bread rationing introduced for the first time.
1950	Petrol rationing ends.
1952	Tea rationing ends.
1954	All rationing finally removed.

Glossary

AFS	Auxiliary Fire Service. Amateur fire-fighters recruited to assist regular firemen with the expected increase in fire due to air raids.
ARP	Air Raid Precautions, later known as Civil Defence.
ATS	Auxiliary Territorial Service.
Austerity	Deprivation, going without or being short of things.
Baedeker raid	German bombing raid on one of Britain's tourist centres selected from the famous Baedeker guide book.
Black-out	Covering all windows, skylights and so on at night-time, so that houses' lights could not be seen from outside.
Boffin	Scientist.
By-election	An election in a single constituency.
Cabinet	The twenty or so leading government ministers.
Call-up	Conscription.
Capitalist	Someone believing in free market enterprise.
Censorship	The limitation of freedom of speech, for example in newspapers, books, or on the radio.
Censure	To disapprove of strongly and criticize something or someone.
Coalition	A government made up of members of more than one political party.
Conscription	Compulsory military service.
Controversial	Disputed.
D-Day	The day the Allies landed in France (6 June 1944).
Deprivation	Going without, suffering from hardship.
ENSA	Entertainments National Service Association; an organization which was supported by the government and which provided entertainment for the forces and factory workers.
Evacuation	Removing people from one place to another.
Führer	Leader.
GI	An American conscript, from 'Government Issue'.
Home Guard	A volunteer force trained to resist German invasion.
Internment	The restriction of someone to a camp or similar limited area.
Land Army	The people who helped keep farming and agriculture going during the war.
Left wing	Inclined towards socialism.
Luftwaffe	German air force.
Ministry	A government department.
Morale	Spirit and confidence.
MP	A Member of Parliament.
Munitions	Weapons and ammunition.
Nazi	A member of the German National Socialist Party.
Order Paper	The day's agenda for the House of Commons.
Pacifist	Someone who does not believe in fighting as a way of settling disputes.
Panzer division	German armoured division.
POW	Prisoner of war.

Propaganda	Information designed to help or hinder a cause.
Rationing	Limiting goods (such as food, clothing) to ensure their fair and equal distribution.
Reich	The German empire.
Requisitioned	Compulsorily acquired by the government.
Unprecedented	Entirely new; something which has never occurred before.
WAAF	Women's Auxiliary Air Force.
Welfare State	The system in which the state undertakes to look after the general welfare (health, education, employment and so on) of all citizens.
WRNS	Women's Royal Naval Service.
WVS	Women's Voluntary Services for Civil Defence.

Further reading

Topic books

Briggs, S., *Keep Smiling Through*, Fontana, 1976.
Calder, A., *People's War*, Panther, 1971.
Cantwell, J.D., *Images of War*, HMSO, 1989.
Gilbert, M., *Second World War*, Weidenfeld, 1989.
Harrison, T., *Living through the Blitz*, Collins, 1976.
Johnson, S.B. (ed.), *The Evacuees*, Gollancz, 1968.
Longmate, N., *The Real Dad's Army*, Hutchinson, 1974.
Marwick, A., *The Home Front*, Thames and Hudson, 1976.
Smith, G., *How it was in the War*, Pavilion, 1989.
Speer, A., *Inside the Third Reich*, Weidenfeld, 1970.
Wicks, B., *The Day They Took the Children*, Bloomsbury, 1989.

Reference books

Chamberlin, E.R., *Life in Wartime Britain*, Batsford, 1972.
Chronicle of the Twentieth Century, Longman, 1988.
Longmate, N., *How We Lived Then – A History of Everyday Life During the Second World War*, Hutchinson, 1971.
Pope, S., Taylor, J. and Wheal, E., *A Dictionary of the Second World War*, Grafton, 1989.
Taylor, A.J.P., *English History 1914–1945*, OUP, 1965.
World War II (many volumes), Time Life Books.

Original sources

Hillary, R., *The Last Enemy*, Pan, 1975.
Waugh, E., *Men at Arms*, Penguin, 1975.
Westall, R., *Children of the Blitz*, Viking, 1985.

Notes on sources

1 Personal interview.
2 *Ourselves in Wartime*, Odhams, n.d., pp. 241–2.
3 Cited in Macdonald, C.K., *Second World War*, Blackwell, 1984, p. 34.
4 Cited in Gibson, R. and Nichol, J., *Germany*, Blackwell, 1985, p. 42.
5 Cited in Macdonald, p. 47.
6 Westall, Robert (ed.), *Children of the Blitz*, Viking, 1985, p. 34.
7 Personal interview.
8 *Ourselves in Wartime*, p. 11.
9 Stevenson, J., *British Society 1914–1945*, Penguin, 1984, p. 449.
10 Stevenson, p. 447.
11 Stevenson, p. 448.
12 *Ourselves in Wartime*, p. 31.
13 Longmate, N., *How We Lived Then – A History of Everyday Life During the Second World War*, Hutchinson, 1971, p. 340.
14 *Daily Express*, 31 May 1940, p. 4.
15 Longmate, p. 81.
16 Westall, p. 149.
17 Westall, p. 155.
18 *Daily Mirror*, 30 August 1940, p. 8.
19 Stevenson, p. 134.
20 Westall, p. 149.
21 *Chronicle of the Twentieth Century*, Longman, 1988, p. 546.
22 *Ourselves in Wartime*, p. 38.
23 Longmate, p. 341.
24 Longmate, p. 337.
25 Cited in Westall, p. 116.
26 Personal interview.
27 *Daily Herald*, 16 November 1940, p. 1.
28 Cited in Shirer, W.L., *The Rise and Fall of the Third Reich*, Simon and Schuster, 1960, pp. 1008–9.
29 Shirer, pp. 1009–10.
30 Taylor, A.J.P., *The Second World War*, Hamish Hamilton, 1975, p. 175.
31 Pierre, M. and Wievionka, A., *The Second World War*, Wayland, 1989, p. 19.
32 A popular phrase in 1938–9.
33 Personal interview.
34 Longmate, p. 93.
35 Cannadine, David (ed.), *Blood, Toil, Tears and Sweat: Winston Churchill's Famous Speeches*, Cassell, 1989, p. 149.
36 Cited in Chamberlin, E.R., *Life in Wartime Britain*, Batsford, 1972, p. 161.
37 Longmate, p. 481.
38 Cited in Mosley, Leonard, *The Battle of Britain*, Time Life, 1977, p. 194.
39 Foot, M.R.P., *Resistance*, Eyre Methuen, 1976, p. 319.
40 Westall, p. 161.
41 Chamberlin, p. 158.
42 Personal interview.
43 Westall, p. 224.

Index

Picture acknowledgements

The author and publishers would like to thank the following for allowing their illustrations to be used in this book: Centre for the Study of Cartoons and Caricature, University of Kent, Canterbury/Solo Sydication and Literary Agency 28, 34 (Low, *Evening Standard*, 15 August 1940); *Daily Mirror* 8; E.T. Archive 22 (top), 42, 44 (bottom), 47 (top); John Frost Historical Newspaper Service 19 (bottom), 44 (top), 45; Hulton-Deutsch Collection 6, 12, 16, 35, 37; Imperial War Museum 25 (top), 27 (bottom); The Labour Party Photograph Library 9 (bottom); Peter Newark's Historical Pictures *cover*, 11 (top), 13 (top), 15, 17, 18, 20, 21, 33, 43 (bottom), 48, 54; Popperfoto 9 (top), 32, 40, 41, 49; Punch 46; Topham 4, 5 (left, right), 7, 11 (bottom), 13 (bottom), 14, 19 (top), 22 (bottom), 23, 24, 25 (bottom), 26, 27 (top), 30 (top, bottom) 36, 38, 39, 43 (top), 47 (bottom), 50, 51 (top, bottom), 53, 55. The artwork was supplied by Euromap Limited.

940.54

DATE DUE

withdrawn 5/3/24

GAYLORD   PRINTED IN U.S.A.